SCATTERED
SYLLABLES

SCATTERED
SYLLABLES

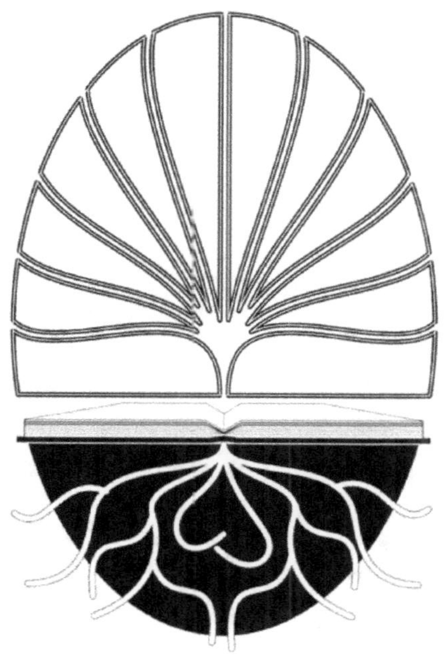

LINDA LOKHEE

An Ink Gladiators Press® Publication

Ink Gladiators Press®
Publishing and promoting warriors on life's battlefield

Ink Gladiators Press® is an ePublishing company whose mission is to publish and promote writers, poets, lyricists, artists and photographers through our current worldwide market distribution of over 3 billion readership. It is not affiliated with any other organization and is an independent ePublishing house. For Earthians who want to publish with us, check out our ongoing publishing opportunities at Our Earthians Community Group, or write to us to learn more about our Celestial Sky Services at our email address: contact@inkgladiatorspress.com.

First Edition
Copyright © Linda Lokhee 2021

Scattered Syllables

ISBN 978-81-949418-9-7

Ink Gladiators Press®
Bangalore, India
www.inkgladiatorspress.com

Credits:
Cover Art & Logo Design - Creozoe
Cover & Book Layout Design - Leonie Belle Hawk
Editor-in-Chief – Reena Doss
Assistant Editor – Preethi Doss

This book is dedicated to my wonderful husband J
and our two sons—N and H—who have been a constant source of joy in my life
and are always encouraging me to write poetry and stories.
Thank you for supporting my dreams of becoming
a picture book author and published poet!
All the poems about family and love are for you.

To my dear mum and late dad, my mother and father-in-law,
my big brother, and beautiful friends—thank you for your endless support.

A special thank you to my best friends, Anna Wainwright and Claudine Everitt
for their guidance, foresight and support,
much earlier than when this poetry light was lit.
They saw my love of writing and knew
that this was the journey I was supposed to be on.

With love and gratitude always.

Table Of Contents

Foreword

Boundless in range, Linda Lokhee is an Olympian athlete and exuberant performer when it comes to writing genres of current events and modern themes.

The Sock Monster was such a joy to read. Ike is a big-eyed, adorable purple monster meant for children to fall in love with. As an adult, I completely fell in love with him too and sent Linda a fun character illustration of Ike (she loves receiving fan art so if you love any of her pieces or picture books, you definitely should)! The genius behind his character is clearly a revelation of beautifully wrapped themes on family, acceptance, friendship, understanding and love.

Her poetry on Instagram is in itself an independent aspect of her writing talent. Her ability to illuminate darkness and showcase the hidden, gives creativity and positivity a different name for all types of age groups. Also, she has recently released her second children's book—*The Night Noise* quite successfully and I am looking forward to reading that next.

A staunch upholder of both mental health and kindness, Linda is deliberately vocal on all media platforms. Using her voice and words to speak, she tackles tough subjects that are not often talked about. Her pieces on racism, gender, equality, climate change, politics, injustice, etc. are intended to cause a reaction while simultaneously inspiring action. The Founder of Feel Good Feb (FGF) and Kindness Is Catching (KiC), Linda takes steps to create mental health awareness through little acts of kindness. She is not only someone who uses her words alone but actually measures them through her actions. FGF spreads kindness within the international community but KiC reaches out to her local community by getting them involved in providing basic necessities and clothes to help the homeless sleep more comfortably during the long winter.

How we met is rather an interesting one and goes back a couple of years ago. I had just joined Instagram in late 2018 and I was really nervous about putting my work out there. Linda was one of the first people I met who generously supported my writing and took the time to get to know me better. Later on, I realized that this is who she is. If she doesn't like something, she is straightforward about it. Everyone is uniquely special to her and she does not waste time with her words because she says exactly what she means.

To me, Linda is one of the most radiating and fascinating personalities on Instagram. How she manages to transmit her light energy to others, yet makes time for her beloved family, friends, local and international community and herself, I will never know. She is accepting of all kinds of people and this translates in her own assorted writing style. She will always have a special place in my heart for I consider her to a woman of exceeding possibilities and know that she is truly one of a kind.

When you pick up Scattered Syllables to add to your collection, know that you will be glimpsing inside the window of a rare sunflower whose hues are not just yellow, but filled with abundant variety and many shades of hope. Treat it gently and I guarantee that you will find a friend within, someone who will personally hold your hand through the scrambled parts of life and comfort you as you grow and learn how to love unconditionally.

God bless you all!

Reena Doss @reenadossauthor
Founder | Ink Gladiators Press®
www.inkgladiatorspress.com

Preface

What started out as a personal challenge has become a lifelong love and what started out as a hobby has become a vocation.

I joined Instagram just before I published my debut children's picture book, The Sock Monster. It was here that I came across my first poetry challenge, a "poem a day" using given words on a day, or a specific poetry form. I thought that I would try and write for this poetry challenge for one week. I discovered that I found writing to word prompts and forms very interesting, so on I went, setting myself the challenge to do another poem a day, for two weeks. By the end of two weeks, I had fallen in love with poetry and the various themes that found themselves into my writing, being sourced from real life and from pure imagination. I decided to finish the poem a day challenge for the month, and yes, I became addicted to writing every single day! The challenge I set myself was to continue past the month and write a poem every day for 100 days. I am happy to say that those 100 days were life changing. After successfully writing 100 poems consecutively, using prompts, and many different poetry styles, I decided to host writing prompts of my own.

Over the years I have set regular monthly poetry word prompt challenges, different unusual writing and visual picture challenges. I have created my own original poetry forms, published on my Instagram wall which people have used to write poetry. This has made me happy and proud to read the creative writings of people from around the world!

I continue to support and highlight the joys of poetry on Instagram by using prompts and sharing poetry on my wall and in my stories. I share poetry that people have written, using my monthly prompts, challenges and original forms. These can be found under hashtag names such as #lokhee3, #lokheeflip4, #lokheelow5 and #lokheecolours.

Over the years, I've entered into many poetry competitions, where I have proudly placed first, second and third. For an international poetry competition run by publisher A.B. Baird Publishing, I was honoured to have won first runner up three times in three years.

In 2019, my poetry was accepted into a poetry anthology. This book, Gratitudes: To Our Mothers, was the first poetry book that began the road into my writing career as a published poet. To date, I am the proud co-author of thirteen poetry anthologies.

I've had fun co-authoring these wide-themed poetry anthologies over the last couple of years. Along with many positive experiences in writing competitions, I've had the confidence to write my own debut poetry collection, Scattered Syllables. I'm so happy that my writing journey has blossomed, and I've been given the opportunity by Ink Gladiators Press to present you with my debut poetry book.

The writing journey will continue for me as a children's book author and a poetess, and I'm excited to be on this path!

Part One

SCATTERED

Who am I? An empty vessel of crimson blood running through my veins, mapping out an original story.

Scattered Contents

I
GRIEF

*Am I an embodiment of a life that was lived
or a connection by those I have loved?*

Life Heist

Alzheimer's, the thief
Creeping
slowly
silently
without a sound
Claiming pieces of you
little by little

Falling away
from oneself
Falling away
from family
Falling away
from life
Fading
incognito
surreptitiously

It didn't ask to take you
It just stole you away
quietly…

Absence

Although I can't touch you anymore
I feel your hand on mine
for when I close my eyes
you're here through this turbulent time

Although I can't hear you now
your advice rings in my head
solid guidance I now recall
a truthful life was led

Is absence a tangible thing?

Your gentle manner floats back to me
fair and firm timbre all your own
words, laughter and sighs
blessed memories hold your tone

Although I can't see you here
my thoughts can recognise
the glimpses of twinkles that shine
in your sweet grandchildren's eyes

Is absence a tangible thing?

You're absent now
a loss felt in times of solitude
always remembered, we were graced
by your generous, selfless attitude

You're absent now
but your life has left an aura tint
a brighter hue lives on instead
an indelible love imprint

Is absence a tangible thing?

Forever Young

I still think of you, my friend
and reminisce on fun times gone by
Laughing at your silly jokes
true friendship not needed to simplify

For when that news came
seems I'd known you a lifetime
Your family and mine so close
all our lives intertwined

The disease was unexpected
paired with a shock so cruel
All our rage at first
towards it, was our fuel

No reason for the attack
on your lungs that were so young
So quickly you fell victim
down life's ladder unwillingly swung

You left way too soon
our hearts broke that day
The pieces of us here
will cherish your bright ray

Time has ticked by
yet you're not in the past
You're here in our memories
still alive, forever to last

I hear you in your son's laugh
I see you in your daughter's eyes
A flash of what we shared
sometimes takes me by surprise

True friendship never dies
perhaps now it's put on hold
You, forever young
while we're left to grow old

You're thought of often
for hearts have a healing design
Oh, how I wish that cancer
was just a simple star sign

Only The Good Die Young

When moonlight graces
the tips of waves
it moves in harmony
like a swaying blanket
The seafarer searches
amongst the lapping waves
for his one true love
lost amongst the flood washed rocks
many a time ago

A mermaid appears
offering a heart trinket to this sailor
but he somehow knows
it's a trick
this isn't her
his one true love

And he will keep searching
this vast ocean forevermore
knowing with aching sadness that
only the good die young

II
HEARTBREAK

I have taken pieces of you and of me;
I know how I have become who you see.

Betrayal

Betrayal is devastating
surprising with a twist
because I never knew
the knife was already in

Blinded

I hear the ringing of your absence
those bells are like assassins
Come to kill the passion
of what was you and me
what we were, was, meant to be...

An empty kitchen with only one mug

I knew you, the way you took your coffee
and the sleepy morning kiss
Is this what you miss?
Light banter over breakfast
or the whirlwind of arguments' tempest?

That wasn't fair

Wish you'd given me a chance
to see what was coming
but your communication was running
No alternate ways to go forward
for into that girl's arms—your reward

Betrayed by both

A three pact where I was blindsided
there's no excusing the both of you
Friendship, love cut right through
You each took a piece of me
and brutally severed it completely

Confused with no answers

Cut out and cast adrift
because you left no forwarding address
Just me in a lonely mess
and you in the arms of someone new

The sting and hurt has left me askew

Regret

Regret for this
for what I've done
Sorry is no good
Not going to beg
but I miss waking up
in a messy knot of arms and legs

You haunt my thoughts
every moment silent
Behind my eyes
in my mind
entwined breaths
this is our bind

I know it's time to end
we've tried it twice before
but our love just hits the floor
and now…
you're showing me the door

Missed Chance

Listen to the ruby rumble
from skies of orange tangerine
Unexpected droplets tumble
he whispers, as wet hits windscreen

But as the mirthful noise splats, she cannot hear
'cause of the breath of the wild
She turns away and leaves the car
not knowing he'd said 'I love you'
these words left unfiled

Three little words
drowned out by the rain
and scattered to the skies
She, heart full of pain
walks away thinking that
love has been a disguise

Gone, Again

I don't understand
how you can cut all ties
just like that
Was our past and laughter all lies?

Did you build us on
sticks and hay?
Temporary lodging
with me halfway?

I didn't realise
you planned to leave
or was it unintentional
our relationship cleaved?

Didn't realise you were
that type of guy
who quickly moved on
without saying goodbye

I mistakenly thought
we knew each other well
You'd confided to me
that you've been through hell

I knew your past
your scars ran deep
You opened up
your blood did seep

So I think you ran
because we got too close
and you faded away
just like a ghost

I knew this was a pattern
of how it always went
The fear of letting someone in
created panic with no vent

But I didn't think you'd repeat it
not with me, surely not?
I had everything to offer you
but rejection was all I got

So I'm left here wondering why

Did I do something wrong
to make you up and leave?
This reaction oh, so strong

In the fear of being hurt
you misjudged our love true
and decided to repeat the pattern
of which you always knew

I'm not going to chase you
I'll let you travel away
I wish you love and luck
and hope you'll come back one day

Where Are You?

We ride on the tips of stars
always spinning, never touching
Missing you, each a piece apart
Are you there in the darkness?

Like a barren tree stripped of all its leaves
this change of season has fallen upon us
our leaves never to share the same branch again
Are you there in the darkness?

Our hearts still beat, yet not together
tied to the winds to reach you
Thoughts drifting, midnight thoughts
Are you there in the darkness?

Notes

Why did my heart break
when you turned your back and left
walking away forever?

Now I listen for
summer on the radio
Warm notes remind me of you

The Lure

No one believed the maiden existed
I saw beauty bloom from depths of the sea
Green eyes captured heart
though mind resisted
for scales glistened brightly
where legs should be!

Under the silver starred sky, I sat on deck
From waves that lapped music of beauty
came the sweet sound of her voice
and through tune she beckoned
Entranced, I forgot
my night watchman's duty

Prepared to jump ship towards her embrace
red hair enticing me nearer
On jagged rock she reached
I forward paced
but was grabbed back by sailors
who didn't hear her

Suddenly awake and broken from trance
saved just in time from sea maiden's death dance

Dream Lover

Dance with me in temporary starlight
treat our feet to open skies delight!
Let crescent moons shine be witness true
to the limitless love between me and you

Kiss me under star clusters bright
our hearts orbiting attraction ignite!
Clasp hands and wander in time distortion
bathe in stars and love's absorption

Alas, the dark brightens and moon retreats
my night-time lover's not within my sheets
We kissed only under the parentheses of dreams;
for when my eyes opened,
you remained
trapped
on moonbeams

III

DEPRESSION

Beneath blue waves, where darkness hides,
what whispers lie inside the chest?

Cloud

I watch the cloud descend on you
sometimes striking fast
like a flash of lightning
other days approaching slowly
an impending storm
at times encompassing you
and I wait
helpless as the darkness seeps

Damp fog—
how can water droplets be so heavy?

You shrink away from me
from my touch, my words
and I am painfully aware
that I'm no umbrella for you

Unwell

Imploding physical world collision
mind mental horrors, self-derision
What is true? She's so confused
her energy sapped, she's been abused
Back and forth, the lies abound
believing every single wicked sound
'til on the floor a crumpled heap
begging for that slither of sleep
but even with eyes tightly closed
upon eyelids come scenes of woe
Stop! Cease! There's no escape!
Mind sealed closed
with imagined tape

She's Still There, Somewhere

I tried…
to entice her with
bursts of bright pink macaroons
and ruby red raspberries
but deeper into bed she would sink

I tried…
to encourage her with
a purpose to get up, to rise
tissues offered like white flags
to soak up the tears in her eyes

I tried…
to infuse her with
my desire, my love, my care
but she turned away
and my heart was stripped bare

I tried…

Immobile

(a Quatern form poem)

Shadows descend, night after night
there's blackness where the light should be
gripped tightly in depression's fight
no space for love, obscurity

Strength wanes and slips, oozing away
shadows descend, night after night
moonlight does nothing to allay
the fears of disappearing light

Outward run from internal height
the drop to deep depths of despair!
Shadows descend, night after night
my soul squeezed tightly, no repair!

Panic ablaze as head shuts down
anxiety taking full flight
and as the cold ices my heart
shadows descend, night after night

Voices

Don't cry! Man up!
they all used to say
The voices in my head
won't let pain go away
so inwards I retreat
burying many secrets deep
until they come to haunt at night
in my bedded sleep

Then tears spill out
with flooded desperation
My guilt pricked body
soaked in perspiration
Shadows haunting mind
sneakily peering in
hooded ghosts to remind me
of my every sin

IV
DOMESTIC VIOLENCE

Reality was fractured, torn and broken;
existence was a jigsaw in pieces.

Spiral

His eyes drew me in
mesmerized by the passion of falling
I tumbled
deeply drawn together
like a magnet, I could not resist
Forgetting all else
in a daze of all things him
But the story changed
darkness seeped in
glimpses of the real him
of misdirected passion now
of red-hot anger
of blame and accusations
until I neither knew myself
nor him
Floating in a bewildered cloud
of uncertainty and guilt
of which I came to believe

Then
a switch back
to the one I knew
beautiful eyes again
and whispered apologies
Promises and I fell again
a Ferris wheel of joy
exhilaration of emotion
but not at the top for long
before
the downward spiral of
black rage and a cloud of hate
of twisted words and raised hands
pieces of me chipped away
Then on the up
heartfelt sorries and eyes that wept
Forgiveness
the pull of him
undeniable
back again
all better…

until the next time

Like A Mask

You portrayed yourself as
the sentry of the sun
blonde, dazzling, words like honey
and eyes like diamonds

Two strangers
with high ideas
hopes to save the world
But after I fell for you
you changed, quick to anger
Your false make-up fell away
barbed words sprung from your throat
like violets and voodoo dolls
sharp pins, causing pain

And the sun fell from the sky
descended, and dark

Clarity

Those words out of your mouth
were like a thousand pinpricks with no relief
My whole body became a pincushion
that screamed in disbelief
An internal storm of thunder
with rainclouds bursting from the inside out

The big questions that followed everywhere
relentlessly intruding into days and nights
were the whys and hows and Oh! The pain!
A confusion that the world just wasn't right
and these feelings of self-doubt

But when the chaos cleared, and you were gone
I realised then
I was the jewel
and you, with your cheating heart
were
quite simply
a fool

Fire Can Burn

This man is like fire
intriguing with his mesmerising flickers
with the promise of warmth
comfort and passion

But fire can burn
unpredictable and changeable to the wind
searing to touch
and reducing me to ash

House of Cards
(a Duplex form poem)

O' come find me in the ruins love
my heart broken in sharp shards, lies scattered

There in sharp shards, your lies are scattered
better separated so as to disguise

Separate to disguise a love that shines
a love that shines bright, so blindingly

Love is blinded so sharp memories are dulled
menacing memories dulled by your sun

Laughter and smiles delivered by the sun
which builds brick by brick, a solid home

A solid home for my head, my heart, my soul
I yearn for a future with you

Future with you was promised, but broken again
O' come find me in the ruins love

V

FEAR

When heartbeats quicken and the mind races,
who is going to help me? Just breathe.

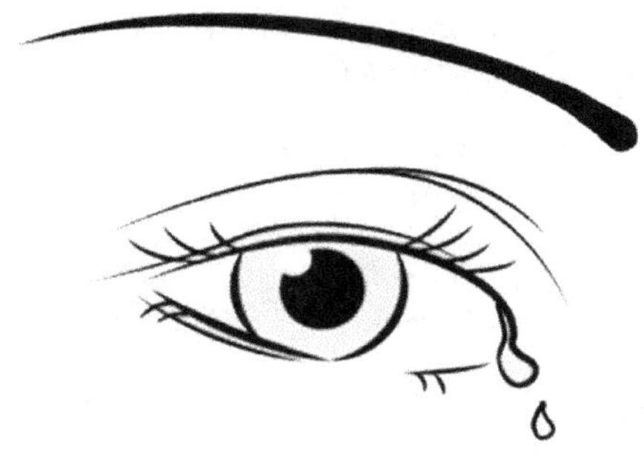

My Name is Fear

I am the shadow that resides
deep in the darkest crevices of your mind
I'm small, I'm hidden, I'm silent
but your insecurities, I'll find

You'll underestimate me
forget about me, push me aside
I'm the niggling feeling
that quiver, the shiver
that lives inside

I snuggle against your heart
and piggyback your thoughts
for the arrogance in me is strong
I like to leave you distraught

Have I made myself clear?

My
name
    is
Fear

Nyctophobia

When inked black night erases light
absence of colour echoes uncertain
The dance between obsidian and opal ripples
as moonlight filters through a dusty curtain

It's All Hallows' Eve and he's uneasy
feeling growing panic, beads of sweat
Can't shake the intuitive feeling
of danger not yet met

Fighting urges of nyctophobia
he switches on the light
Looks around, there's no one there
and pulls the covers up tight

Mouth still dry like sandpaper
heart thumps chest, a runaway drum
"There's no one here," he says aloud
and waits anxiously for sleep to come

He closes eyes but feels the urge
to flick them open for a peek
'cause he feels the prickle on his neck
and fear begins to seep

"There's no one here," he says aloud
the drums become a roar
He starts to shake, his toes exposed
the sweat begins to pour

"There's no one here…
no one here…
one here…
…here!"

VI
COMMUNITY

Humanity thrives on diversity and love.

Homeless

There's a spot I sit at
each morning, every day;
my back to the railing
face turned to warm sun rays

People hurry past
faces to phones
ignoring my cup
and that I'm all alone

My history, my past
they don't know or care
what I've been through
or how I've gotten there

My wife, my child
my job, my home
all disappeared…
the streets I now roam

My belongings, now bundled
I'm dependent on charity
I live day by day
with no future clarity

I may not have much
but I'm still me
Don't just pass by
please don't ignore

I'm much more than what you see

The Hoarder

He collects things
They sit, build, squash
He can't let them go
Meaningful moments
sentimental stirrings
Newspapers from long ago
ticket stubs, jam jars
empty perfume bottles
boxes from Christmas' past
Attached to a life lived
and to a life loved
in messy order
Maybe there's a crazy wisdom
in a *hoarder's* life

The Escalator to the Casino

Metal stairs, upwards to temptation
Heart beating, hating the sensation
but she can't help it, moving towards the lights—
to machines, gunshot bleeps, money it bites!
Can't anyone see? It's not a predilection
She's smart, she's knows it's an addiction
Nearly up there, the buzz is real
Maybe this time, the jackpot she can feel…
Wishing one day she could stop—
the familiarity hypnotises, almost to the top
Feed the machine her money, pull the pole
Feed the machine, her secret, her coins, her soul

Displaced
(a Loop form poem)

What do you tell a child?
Child we have to leave home
Home where your bed is and all you have
Have you got your Teddy?
Teddy will comfort you when you're scared
Scared I am of bullets outside
Outside where there's violence and intimidation
Intimidation from those who seek
Seek to persecute us for our beliefs
Beliefs of a different religion or ethnicity
Ethnicity of which we are born
Born into a world of war you are
Are you terrified, my little one?
One day we will be safe
Safe in a place which means us no harm
Harm, horror, tears for years are all I know
Know this, my child, I love you
You in my heart won't be displaced
Displaced

Why?
(a Terzanelle form poem)

Why does this keep happening now?
Random violence causing pain
protect our people, make a vow!

Stone memorials list their names
souls cry out in pure innocence
random violence causing pain

Politicians rest on the fence
pointing fingers, "Who's to blame?"
Souls cry out in pure innocence

Anguished families not the same
grief struck, broken, tear-stained and lost
pointing fingers, "Who's to blame?"

Freedom lives on, but at what cost?
Campaign for change must happen soon
grief struck, broken, tear-stained and lost

Prevent chaos, we're not immune!
Why does this keep happening now?
Campaign for change must happen soon
Protect our people, make a vow!

The Game of Life

Yes
For those who fight
the constant injustices in the world

No
For the relentless publicity searchers
those who whirl and twirl for fame

Yes
To the faceless peacekeepers,
silently endeavouring for justice
behind the scenes

No
To duplicitous faces
who escape reality through
the meaningless crush of words

Yes
For courage, tall values and people
whose priorities lie in peace

Which *Game of Life* do you live in?
I'm out of my mind watching this

endless

game

of

World

Ping Pong

VII
DISASTER AND DISEASE

Relentless destruction left in their wake,
with all crying, how much more will they take?

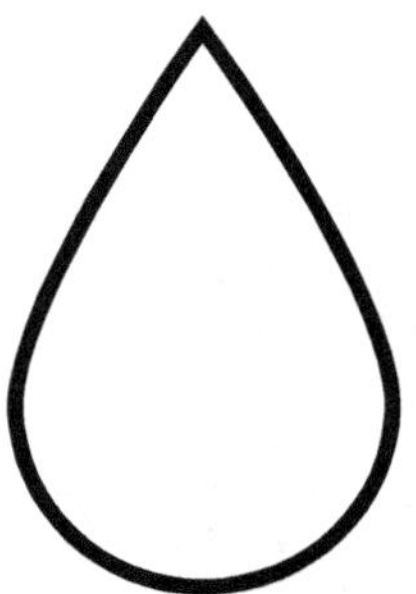

Our Missing Moon

Who has seen our missing gold moon?
She's shrouded in a scarlet hood
swaying in the smoke-hazed dune
alone and misunderstood

Who has seen our missing gold moon?
She weeps silent tears in musty light
for the land below is cast maroon;
shades of raging red and choking graphite

Who has seen our missing gold moon?
She shimmers, she's still there
behind the piercing red veil, she swoons
and waits for the rain to repair

Burnt

Burnt razor red
their whole world is on fire
into unknown danger led

Smoky haze
hear blankets of snapping twigs
firefighters' struggled daze

Heroic
courageously fighting flames
dangerously like world's end

When the Flames Died Down

You can't see the flames rising high
hear the roar of blaze in the sky
or taste the ashy charcoal leaves
but
do not be deceived
for
the evidence is obvious in twists

In the dulled grey blanketed mist
where no discernible line lies
between sky and ocean's eye
and
the bushfire fallout gives it away
to burnt black amongst the sea spray

Corona Virus
(a Triquint form poem)

Pandemic sweeps, a virus pinwheel
panic lines, nation's newsreel
Swift pain can't conceal
all too real
Tear

Victims' families cry an appeal
prayers to God to make a deal
Swift pain can't conceal
all too real
Fear

Forced lockdowns, work shutdowns, so surreal
vaccine's timelines not ideal
Swift pain can't conceal
all too real
Here

Part Two

GROWING

*Travel through life not bound by a road map
but with wings of creation.*

Growing Contents

I
IMAGINATION

Find a space to soar and move, to be limitless and create.

Mermaid

Sometimes I wish I could
show the world my mermaid tail
But would you recoil in surprise
or be disgusted by my disguise?

Would you scream at my scales
or want to touch my tail?
Are you curious about my deception
or do you respect my inception?

I've called on courage and strength
keeping secret pretence at length
Yes, fake legs appearing on demand
walking around the dry land

But home in the deep sea
I'm content to be me

Magic

On a cool day
at the end of spring
the leaves sparkled
and the clouds did sing

Another fairy
would enter the land
with magical waters
and gifted hands

With sweet essence
she brought forth light
No more hiding
things would be set right

With a twist of her smile
and glimmering eyes
this fairy was in
for a big surprise

Lilac stars filled the sky
hidden behind the sun
waiting patiently
for the night to fall

Inching closer,
they whispered a plan....

Niftily shifting stars
whilst   watching below
as faeries danced and sang
and younglings skipped in glee

When celebrations concluded
and dusk descended like an ebony blanket
the guest of honour
looked up and saw the stars' gift
They'd formed the words—
I K I G A I

Hidden Worlds

Every book is a door
each page will invite you in
Wander around and explore
escape from the outside din
Imaginations will fill
other worlds giving thrills
suspense and mysteries within

Let the hours tick away
as immersion fills your time
Words and adventures interplay
get lost in books' paradigm
Caught up 'til the moon shines high
shocked to see that time does fly—
wishing in pages to stay...

II
DON'T GIVE UP

Calmly breathe, keep reaching skywards
and trust that we are all connected.

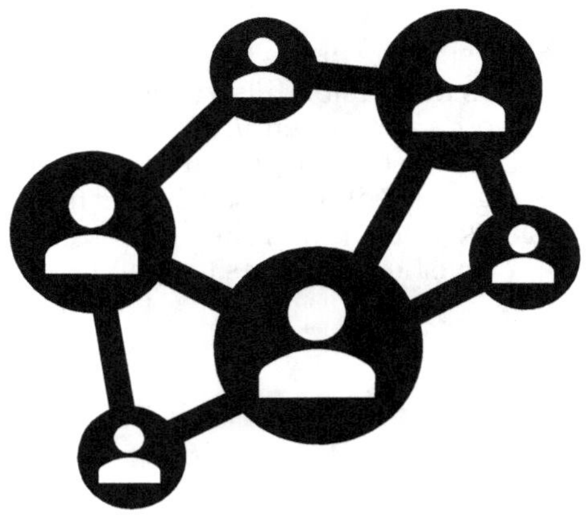

Thunderbird Eggs

They called me ugly
with a mottled hard exterior
Dull and brittle
something to be overlooked

But what they didn't know
was that I shone
like a diamond inside
despite my cracks

Stars

Stars on their strings
dangling within reach

Stars on their strings
climbing with broken wings
but still
upward goals we beseech
never muzzled
freedom of speech

Stars on their strings
dangling within reach

Look For The Light

No one guiding, floating alone
constellations misaligned, future unknown

Turning, turning
blackness, despair
confusion in bones, no repair

But wait…
One little spark blinking faintly
amongst the dark

Move towards it, gravitate
There's always hope
don't hesitate

Gentle pull, not stuck in a bind
There's always light, free your mind

The Strength

How can I pay these bills
when my job comes to a close?

*I will go on with mountain's strength behind
my face to fluid sea*

How do I move
when there's airborne virulent particles?

*I will go on with mountain's strength behind
my face to fluid sea*

How can I face the future
when a friendship abruptly ends?

*I will go on with mountain's strength behind
my face to fluid sea*

How do I cope
when you've taken one half of my blistered heart?

*I will go on with mountain's strength behind
my face to fluid sea*

How? How? How?

*I will go on with mountain's strength behind
my face to fluid sea*

Blooming

From a singed heart, she delves
last moonlit sigh releases
with the sweetest breath
of incandescent innocence
beginning a trail to healing

In the effervescent blooms
alighting upwards from within
she spills the secrets
from beyond the known universe
releasing a rush of power

For when the sleeper awakens
she brings forth such inner strength
An instinctive knowingness
that she will survive
and she will thrive

Fighter

How did this Silence get so loud?
Self-doubt and heaviness weighing down
Fattened inky onyx weaving the air
into an unwanted thorny crown

It sits atop, digging and scraping
trying to invade
but all along it's only a passenger
and time will make it fade

For each small step the mind makes
towards the sparks of light
that's offered by small slivers of hope
will break the thorn's sharp bite

Take the love, the advice that's given
by those who love and care
Let it fill the black, replace with colour
so that mind and heart can repair

When Love's light is lit, brightly inside
your bruised heart will start to rise
Healing can begin at last
and darkness will release its ties

The new day dawns and brings a peace
the green of the leaves seem brighter
There's courage in the air you breathe
from the winds whispering that
you're a fighter

One World

Isn't it funny how all around the world...

Red lights mean stop and green means go?
Our grass keeps growing and needs a mow?
We cut ourselves and we will bleed
We can't go long without a feed
The weather's cold, need more clothes?
Sneeze! Want a tissue for your nose?
The weekend comes, can you feel the love?
Rain continues to pour, from up above

Isn't it funny how all around the world...

Kids wake up crying in the night?
In scary movies, do you jump in fright?
Warning signs at swimming holes
Watch Out For Crocs! That's the goal!
Our ocean waves, they won't keep still
Garbage keeps coming, into our landfill

All these things and many more
An infinite number, I can't keep score
We are one world, can you see?
So where's the love for you and me?

One World
One Heart
One Love
One Peace

I wish for all the wars to cease...

Time

Time will measure life's moments

Exam time, tick tock, gone too fast
The agonising slowness of an accident
The rush of a day filled with laughter
The lingering deliciousness of a first kiss

The impatience of time
but also, know that…

Time will mark our last goodbye

Time will treasure life's moments

Reach Out

Benevolence
share hopes

Lend a hand
through simple gestures

Encompass

Sunshine

Stay in touch with that inner voice
Don't close yourself away from you
Troubles point to shutting down
hiding away from people, feeling blue

Ignoring the world
and those who love you
The world becomes obsidian
you feel the crushing dark

But wait…

There's a seed inside you
like a tiny pepita
for there lies
the golden nugget of sunshine

Stay close to people
who feel like sunshine
They'll shine on your pepita
and love will bloom

III
HEALING

Light seeks to mute shadows,
just as each morning rises steadily from the night.

I See You

Though you're shattered, bruised
and holes are in your heart
let me be the one
to place the pieces
back together again
because sweetheart
your light still shines
through those holes
and I can see your goodness
even if
you're in the shadows

Melt the Frost

A killer frost has descended
upon you, my lovely
You're stuck, frozen in time
and wishing to go back to her

Let me be the sun
that melts your pain
and warms your heart
Come with me...

For we have built
a foundation of friendship
You leave clues sometimes
where slipped rays of sunshine peek

Your smile reaches
the recesses of your eyes
when we are together
Trust me...

R U OK?

Your walls go up
you won't stand up
tears pile up!

Self-protection
Disconnection
Self-reflection
Introspection
Seek connection?

Are you there
inside, somewhere?
Hello there,
rekindle connection
R U Ok?

Notes of the Past

The stars shone down like talismans
the moonbeam tracing a path

In the silent sky
he strummed a note
to bridge the void
of fight's aftermath

His voice mesmerised her
as he wove their past into song
gently plucking memories
on the lines of his guitar long

The story of
a lost young girl
eyes darkened
with hidden stars

And with each precious note played
he released the pain of her scars

My Face
(a Fibonacci form poem)

Flaws
face
wrinkles
lines of life
times of joy, sorrow
marking the journey of my life
mirror reflects the understanding of who I am
this world is larger than me and I accept the lessons from harsh wind and
bright sunshine

Unburden

Those who consume
pain and grudges
walk with
anger and hate

Open your heart
to be
released

Memories

My memories of you are stored
in the vast sky of my mind

The good ones shine
with a tail of trailing stars

The bad ones go
to the dark side of the moon

The sun shines and days pass
yet shadows of you
still follow me

The Journey

Who am I?
An empty vessel
of crimson blood
running through veins
mapping an original journey

Am I the embodiment of
a single life lived
or of connection
surrounded
by those I have loved?

I have taken pieces of you
of them, of me
and they were given
through time
through love
and blood
and tears

And now I know
how
I have become who you see
before you

Kill Them With Kindness

Kill them with kindness,
king-size!

Don't dally or demoralise
Ignore ignorant injustices
when vented viciously vocally via vacantness
because fatigued marred silhouettes of souls sprout

Kill them with kindness,
king-size!

Insensitive irrational people can improvise intentional lies
but by believing babbles, you babysit baboons!
Consider communicating confidently, conscious of truth cast in stone
Word fires die as freedom flowers with familiar kindness

Kill them with kindness,
king-size!

Entice empathy, enlisting no disguise
Leave labellers languishing in their labyrinths
Integrate inner peace, influence individuality
Champion compassion and covet change

Kill them with kindness,
king-size!

Slow Down

Mindless chatter
focus, goal orientate
Time is now
to fixate

Listen
to internal rhyme
Know we're on
borrowed time

One thing—
slow down
Life is not
a countdown

IV
FREEDOM

Freedom arrives inside the early sunrise
of being who you feel you were always meant to be.

Being Free

The gratitude of freedom is strong within her
with no bounds of barbed wire limitations
Away from pressing matters of the heart
thoughts floating, living in the moment
Time passing in a gentle flow of green
being still to appreciate the beauty
of this place we call home
Freedom to create
freedom to work
freedom to live
a life so very
LOVED

Remember The Magic

Fairytales reside inside our minds
in our hearts; our soul
As kids we laugh, we cry, we play
as woven magic touches the day

But life moves on...

Tales are crushed in the droll
we are but slaves to the payroll
Blindfolded are we
imagination held captive
Forgetting the fire
the myths now inactive
Awaken your dragon
in the middle of your being
Discover your power
your fairytales are freeing

Uncloak, discover
Invoke your inner fire
Liberate, be free!

Fly Away

Fly away little pretty bird, fly away
Your brilliant mind full of equations
Not easy for you, to just be you
don't conform
to others' persuasions

Fly away little pretty bird, fly away
I love you true, my little sweet one
No one should ever clip your wings
Don't shield your eyes
from the midnight sun

Fly away little pretty bird, fly away
Together we'll sprinkle moonbeams
Shining love anew and solving
any problems
thwarting your dreams

And although I'm fighting
custody battles for you…

It's not for you to worry my child
My heart, my head, my love is true
Please don't cry, I'll hold you tight
Listen to me girl, it's not your fight
You're always safe, with me you'll stay
I know you'll always return
but fly away little pretty bird, fly away

Duality

She stays in shadows, silent
the other me, compliant
for she's shy, her words reliant

Unlike the outer me,
who is defiant

The stronger she, rambunctious
she speaks completely compunctious
losing empathy of words scrumptious

Until the *two MEs* malfunction
mumble tumble conjunction
blur, blend, expunction

Becoming one bird of a feather
we are champions together
Internal, integrate as one we treasure
for a more even *Me*, a pleasure

Just A Circus

Is life a circus?
Some people juggle
the complexities of family
and the stress of work

Whilst others juggle
the tightrope in between—
their vicious minds from within
and the quieting of white noise

Some people juggle
the tenuous scale
of good health between
antibodies and invading viruses

All we can ever wish for
is balance
in this circus of ours
Time juggling
Health juggling
Life juggling

Letter to Four-Year-Old Me

Dear Younger Me,
sweet and pure,
just four years old

Advice from the future:

Listen to those who have willing wisdom
recognise **Gratitude** and show it
Love fiercely with a passion untold
Live this life fully with no regrets

Embrace mistakes made; they are yours to learn
Accept for not all things can be controlled
Speak your truth inside where trust resides
Unharness your heart of wilderness

With every living breath, **Harmony** you must hold
Board your unicorn, girl
this world's going to show you
Magical sights to behold

Keeping all these in sight
go for dreams of gold!

Tattooed Notes On Skin

I will always write
sure as ink runs through my veins
Emotions flowing
stories coursing faithfully
seeping up through my skin

Midnight Ink

Mind of its own
the pen dips & dances
Even coffee can't interrupt
the flow of early morning
compositions
as the sheets bathe
in silken moonlight

V
HOPE

A single daffodil blooms atop a mountain.
Is it lonesome? Nay, because she's closer to the sun.

Hope Always Survives
(a Palindrome form poem)

There!
Hope buried below
Deep down
He searches peeks, peels slowly
scabs covered from times past
Doesn't come easy
Push past the past

because living with shadows is too dark

Past the past—push!
Easy come? Doesn't
Past times from covered scabs
slowly peels, peeks, searches he
Down deep
below buried hope
There!

Choices

Will I remain lost to be?
My heart-cracks
are open
for all to see

Blinded and confused
betrayal cuts deep
Rivers of tears
now none left to weep

Choices ahead
at the path's cross
One way to freedom
the other, I'm lost

So I take a deep breath
and pick up heart's pieces
turn down hope's path
as my old love...
releases

I'll Find You

Spinning particles
always moving
I'm trying to find
a way back to you

You're on a star
my twin flame grooving
lighting up
a trail of clues

The void in between
spinning particles tear
dancing and weaving
to their own sweet tune

So my love, if you want me
I'll be here
ensconced in the nook
of the moon

The Stars' Healing Lullaby

Emerging from the shadows deep
I lie alone as moonlight seeps
An ache familiar fills my chest
returning, an unwelcome guest

Though we are past, love will still creep
emerging from the shadows deep
Memories of our love remain
sweet blanketing to mask the pain

The stars outside begin to sing
notes of hope, enchantment will bring
Emerging from the shadows deep
soft healing lullaby to sleep

Glimmers flutter replacing dark
shoots a tiny happiness spark
Inside my heart—a true faith leap
emerging from the shadows deep

A Silent Strength

She's quiet and still
roots firmly in the ground
beside a babbling brook

She stretches, upward bound

Moment by moment as time passes by
she lengthens and grow
reaching for the sky

She stretches, upward bound

She's quiet and still
roots firmly in the ground
beside a babbling brook

She stretches, upward bound

She stands proudly displaying beauty so pure
azurite, aquamarine
divine messenger assured

She stretches, upward bound

Determination

I want to know what it's like
to stand
at the foot of my problems and say,
*"I will conquer and overcome you
maybe not now, but someday"*

I want to know what it's like
to see
from blessed Angel's above view—
these problems, seemingly insurmountable
reduced in vision to a few.

I want to know what it's like
to hear
my confidence, my inner voice whispering,
*"You're worthy, my darling,
have no fear, there's always a choice"*

I want to know what it's like
to climb
without fighting, I'm too fatigued
Capture my strength to tap
into myself, now I'm left intrigued.

I want to know what it's like
to taste
the situation, to solve and move on.
No problem too big, there's hope
for the future, I'll be strong.

I want to know what it's like
to shout
in fullness of my dreams
with my feet firmly planted
at the summit in glorious victory.

Some Days

Some days the sun will shine
on someone other than you
Some will feel the green monster
biting, somersaulting, assaulting their bellies
and some will feel nothing at all

Somehow don't you think
to feel
something other than jealousy
to feel
some love and happiness
is the best feeling of them all?

Be

My soul longs to be free
to let go and just be me
but now I've realised
to be free
I just have to
Be

Self Confidence

She reaches inside
deep down
she knows her worth
she holds her crown

Though doubt was sown
and eyes were blinded
Always she knew
didn't need to be reminded

That she was *she*
her *self* she accepted
even through the whirl of lies
intercepted

Steadying hand
feet firm
Head held high
her life
on her terms

Immersion

Today I am granted rhapsody
for I have danced
with a fire in my head
listened to a moonlight silhouette city
whispering of untold adventures ahead
transformed into a mermaid on land
not in the silent seas
but oh, so close…

Through the coolness of a painting
I touch
breathe
exhale

With self-friendship residing inside
I walk on to create
tomorrow's memories

VI
HOME

Home is where my heart and head rests in grateful bliss.

Bushfires

(an X-poem form)

The flames lick high   Water fights flames
orange and red   aqua rains down
Destroying all   tries to cover
fierce hell is nigh   to soak the plains
Engulfing life   Wetness on ground
ignores help's call   drops discover
Days into months
flames, water meet
an endless war
Still fire hunts
and droplets greet
quelling its core
Machines and man   The green shall grow
persist and try   where once it bloomed
for all's not lost   Spirits unite
Safety on land   through tales of woe
blackened trees cry   Bright hope resumed
at nature's cost   from this red fight

Fire, Flood, Virus
(a sonnet form poem)

Hath our world sort out to test and terrorise?
Our failure to see future broken plans
Naive world view, reflected in our eyes
War gods contrive as deadly games began

Fires blaze, our lives engulfed in ash burnt smoke
Such courage rumbled deep across the land
Eyes blind, lives lost amidst this orange cloak
Doused by golden stitched rain, this fire brand

Dew drops sparkle as new life awakens
Reprieve? No rest, bouquets of stones cast down
with virulent cocktails stirred and shaken
Again, fight for life, throw off death's dark frown

We've strength to rise now, see this challenge through
Our world's future, we'll fight for freedom true!

Social Isolation
*(Inspired by Kathleen O'Meara's poem,
'And People Stayed Home')*

And people stayed at home
to halt the virus spreading
to protect our most vulnerable citizens
to stop the dominoes of falling bodies
to stem the wavelength of the world's timeless turmoil
to protect each other
People cried
people despaired
people prayed
people hoped
and people bonded together
and people talked
through board games and forced family lockdowns
A world community fighting an invisible enemy
and time races on
and they take it day by day
and listen to the news breaking
and fears about life lessen
and medication notes the march of civilisation
and people smile as doors once more open, empowered
just as sunshine shines through cobwebs

Slow Down

Do you think you've worried enough?

True, we've got rules to keep us in place
but now these rules we should embrace
Social isolation keeps more people alive
I'll do it if it means that humans will survive

A sacrifice of freedom will pay great dividends

It will give the world a chance to mend
Information streams affecting us all
but we won't let
Covid-19 be our downfall!

Hush hush, slow down…

Quieten your mind
Look at the beauty
in this bird box
the tables have turned
we're now confined

*Will you spend your time
staring at clocks?*

Sydney Vivid Light Festival

There she is
a city within
clear castle walls
waves underpin

Bustled work by day
but come the night
bold, reborn
a festival of light

Ruby key twists
fire heart explodes
hidden life
suddenly exposed

No cloudy skies
now primrose and plum
proud shout and shine
of colours from glum

She's overjoyed
and celebrating
life, love
and happiness pulsating

Gold, silver, rainbow
sparkles she'll wear
a truly royal city
of fun she'll declare

Grab happiness and dance
be luminous and bright
feel your power within
release your inner sprite

New Year's Eve in Sydney

Iridescent prints light up the black sky
Panoply of paint splattered up high
On canvas black, a battle of the night
Farewell torpid thoughts, welcome arcs of light

Banish darkness now, let it fall away
Let bygones be gone, spark a new pathway
Look ahead, so much possibility
Perfect time to show flexibility

Embrace the fireworks within your mind
Untangle, let go; redefine, unbind
Colour your year with heartfelt confidence
Go forth, recover your cognizance

City Girl

Heart of my home, my sweet duende
bustling energetic spirit by day
Sydney skyline, the city of hope basks in sunshine
Oh, how I love your street disarray!

But as night-time falls and all is still
a calm descends upon you
Sunshine basks, skyline hope in the city of Sydney
I'm your philocalist, entranced by your hue

You are where my loyalty lies
for I fell in love in your embrace
Sydney skyline, the city of hope basks in sunshine
content and growing in this aeonian place

ANZAC Day

Anzac Day is to remember them—
our courageous servicewomen and servicemen
who with faith, hope, mateship and trust
left their homes to fight for Freedom for us

They landed in Gallipoli in 1915
travelling to a place they'd never even seen
What horrors awaited, in this unknown war
etched in their minds, forevermore?
Sacrifice for our country, paid with their lives
leaving behind bereaved children and wives

On this day 25th April, we stop to commemorate
those in our past, for Australia's history they did shape
All people since, involved in our peacekeeping
we respect and honour those who went truth seeking

Thank you for your bravery
an admirable example forever set
Thank you to our Anzac Legends
Lest we forget

Special Education Artwork Lesson

Masterpieces of art
splattered paint apart

Mixed media glued
colours not subdued

Kids with special needs
creative mind feeds

Hidden sparks of light
diamonds in the night

Participation
Appreciation

Harmony Day

Our world is full of colour
it's bursting at the seam!
But look beyond the obvious—
Aren't we all on the same team?

What matters in this world
is the quality of people

Not the colour of your skin
or what's on the steeple
of your church
or your religion
your beliefs
nor who you love

We're all on this Earth together
so let's rise above

Don't judge on what you see
be quick to squash down our kin
Look underneath the colours
of our hair, eyes and skin

Our world is full of colour
it's bursting at the seam!

Don't discriminate
if we're naturally thin
built bigger
or by our parents' origin

Can we look at our qualities
of kindness, spirit and giving?

Can every day be a Harmony Day
in a world worth living?
Our future generation
becomes what we model to our kids
The future will become our present
They'll all lead our nation
so look beyond the obvious —
Aren't we all on the same team?

VII
MOTHER NATURE

Nature has the best paintbrush for even in times of darkness,
there is beauty in her masterpieces.

A Lavender Glow

There's a tiny window
in the rise of dawn
a certain glow
a day being born

There's magic there
just a spark anew
A creation of dare
in a purple hue

It is hope, it is trust
a courageous nudge
Banish doubt to dust
quash the self-judge!

Listen to you
inside is your power
Now is the time!
It is the violet hour
our world's not a static polaroid

Breath of the Wind

My breath can lift
bird wings so swift
It is my gift
to this sweet world

Through trees I sweep
wake leaves from sleep
Uplift and keep
them moving, swirled

Sometimes when bored
I sharpen my sword
Strike through mind's hoard
your thoughts, I've hurled

Some crave my calm
a healing balm
To soothe away harm
with fresh breath twirled

Radiance

She's power, she's radiant
harnessing the clouds above
Searching light, love's gradient
climbing towards her, ungloved

Sculpting peace, her agenda
she cannot hear the brontide
Humanity's defender
for us, angels walk beside

Absorb the ocean's synergy
Mother Earth, she has provided
Take it in, eyes and heart entwined
Just breathe...
Be grounded, be present
alignment of my soul and mind

Glimpse of an Angel

She strolled through fields of lavender
taking time to be alone
'Twas serendipity to see her
behind the *hua'he*, I was unknown

She was luminous in quiet beauty's glow
exuding ethereal elegance
Calmness spread throughout the meadow
pure love, peace prevailing prevalence

I watched her approach my hiding place
each step, a spiritual path bound
My fear of being found, falling from grace
alleviated as she turned around

There I saw, upon her back folded in
the most breathtaking sight!
Transparent curled wings
fluttering gaily in the light

I believe in magic, wishes and dreams
for there's more to truth than what is seen

Just Breathe

Midnight stillness
except for the ocean waves
White foam advancing through
the canvas of black

I sit…

Cross legged, a human knot
I burrow myself into the grains
using sand as a blanket
The breeze curls around my hair
gently whispering

I wait…

Breathe in the peace
I can almost taste the salt
I look out into a whole world
that lives underwater
that which I'll never know

And I am grounded once again into ours

Ocean's Love

You are my solace
a place that calms and revives
Cover me, my sea

Ocean's Song

Mother Nature, beauty so pure
reflected in your eyes azure
Melodious song through lapping water
eternally grateful, I am Earth's Daughter

Sunlight halo like pure gold spun
rays woven with aqua, love's done!
Bathe in your magnificence, face skyward
soul replenished, my heart is inspired

Your roots may be stalled right now
but as the lotus blooms in the night
so too, shall you rise
abundant and beautiful

Standing along the bank and bridge
where things look still and quiet
But keep a lockout for the boat
which will bring you to your new start

Starfish

Starfish sway
swinging sideways
singing sea shanties
songs so sweet!

Sinking softly
shimmering sand
soaking sunshine
swishing, swishing!

Sparkling

soothing

soulmates…

Earth Hour
(a Butterfly Nonet and Shape form poem)

Mirrored angles and reflections
awareness floats, zephyr winds
Climate change is here, now

The cure is to care
Switch your lights off—
Earth Hour
tonight

Shift

GLOBE

Sustain

Future thoughts
connect to Earth
Protect the planet
Responsibility

Speak up for animal life
I want to see the flowers bloom
preserve our biodiversity

Ode to the Weed

Oh, sweet little sprouting seed
tendrils so young and sweet!

Not knowing yet that you're a weed
you'll be met with disdain

My advice I hope you'll heed—
ignore the haters' prejudice
for then a happier life you'll lead
more fulfilling days you'll meet

Oh, sweet little sprouting seed
tendrils so young and sweet!

May sunshine's rays
sustain your need

Complexities of Woman

An artisan of life is she
thoughts swish around inside her mind
Imagination sparks the sea
an endless turning movement grind

A woman's mind may puzzle men
and keep them at the edge of zen
Yet, treasure her complexity
this goddess is the soul's entity—
the *Tree of Life*

Is the *Tree of Life* Mother Earth?
A rebirth—
growth and change in all directions?
Deep connections safely grounded
as we reach high on land and sky?

We're blessed by angels standing by
free to explore our universe
Fear no challenge we must traverse
a rebirth, deep connections to land and sky

Moon Maiden

Mystic amber moon watches
silently shining her blessings

Lunar light fingers reaching rooms
sweeping across like midnight brooms
Clearing away cobwebs in dreams
carrying worries away on her moonbeams

Mystic amber moon watches
silently shining her blessings

Winter

The songbird flies away
leaving the sparkling water behind
The flow of endless cool movement
is replaced by a sheet of immobility

A toughness of ice

But hardness is just a front
for winter is still kind
Below the surface
the water still flows

A gentle home for creatures

Beyond the frozen water
lay mountains with snow blankets
With divots tracing a snakelike path
top to bottom, skis and boards

Sounds of children's laughter

The snow winks
the sun smiles
There's balance
between nature and life

Winter visits

Autumn

Autumn rudely jumped in
bringing wind and rainy skies
Gone is the sun
How fast summer flies!

No more poolside parties
no more lazing at the beach
no more late-night evenings
no more strawberry picking within reach

Autumn rudely jumped in
tearing leaves from helpless trees
Leaving them in golden puddles
that we'll jump in to our knees

No more naps in hammocks
no more melty ice cream
no more drinks with umbrellas
no more outdoor festival dream

Autumn rudely jumped in
bringing cosy jumpers, fluffy socks
mugs of hot chocky with marshmallows
and crackling fire on charcoal rocks

No more sweaty bodies
no more stinky feet
no more mozzies and flies
no more cricket on repeat

Maybe autumn
isn't so bad after all…

Spring

Spring sun comes around
rays tumble to ground
Mixing with the sodden earth
curious seeds peek
Adventures they seek
reaching upwards for rebirth

Like life and its run
new days born with sun
Dark and empty sets with night
bringing faith and hope
Life is a tightrope

With balance,
head towards the light

Summer

Now summer's breath
blows warmly on our necks
leaving prints of pink as a souvenir
"Remember me!" she gaily laughs outside
as she sprinkles her rays of happiness

The ocean calls out to his sister, *"Come!"*
He loves the golden rays blankety warm
the temperature inviting us to swim
We dive and laugh
riding on froth tipped waves

Ocean's deep blue
mirrors the sapphire sky
an unbroken cloudless painted masterpiece
We dig large moats and create sandcastles
knowing they're going to be jumped on!

Hot fish and chips make our stomachs rumble
Finally amongst the humidity
the smell and crisp crunch of food is alluring
Seagulls swoop
stealing a chip from my hand

Summer in Sydney smiles her approval
Her heat radiates over the city
She rises and sets every single day
content in her power
to bring pure joy

Part Three

LOVE

*Love, you are welcomed here
on my lips, my eyes and in my heart.*

Love Contents

I

BEAUTY

*Mother Nature has a way of displaying true love stories
as outdoor art masterpieces.*

Sunrise

She is a violet hue
running through grey;
with a hint of red
the deepest shade

Certainly a wonderment
beauty is she;
an elegant original
is our sunrise filigree

Her smile enriches
all who receive;
goodness radiates
with the magic she weaves

Craving Sunlight's Crown

There in the valley of shadows cast
lay a meadow of daffodils steeped in shade
Each one perfect
though yearning for sunshine's blast
nestled amongst nature's fragile blade

"Sway my sisters!" they breathed in motion
like silent wind chimes they sang their tune
An abundant sorrow-filled silent notion
of a lilac meadow floral platoon

At first they'd stood, their heads held high
claiming harmony as one
But as the dark descended, made them cry
the stillness of swaying had begun

In twilight dusk
bereft of sounds
and silences blanket
I sighed once more
once more

Starved of light, their direction stunted
for the mountains around
blocked their light
Slowly their will for growth was blunted
their blossom heads keeled, losing the fight

In twilight dusk
bereft of sounds
and silences blanket
I sighed once more
once more

There they stayed, huddled and still
I sent storms with lightning bolts strong
It raged and rained
and cracked trees on the hill
Until a fallen blanket of wood soldiers
lay scattered long

When skies were wiped clean
of Mother Nature's tears
and half the mountainside lay cleared
The sunlight
filtered across the meadow dears
There, golden warm crowns appeared

From that day forth
and long morrows after,
the daffodils danced in delight
Their freedom to grow
brought untainted laughter
For after darkened lockdown
patience was hindsight

*In twilight dusk
bereft of sounds
and silences blanket
I rested once more
once more*

The Beach
(a Palindrome form poem)

Beautiful
natural artwork masterpiece
orange and blue colours
complement
together forever
each puzzle piece
true love story
ocean and sand

everlasting synergy, a perfect match

sand and ocean
story love true
piece puzzle each
forever together
complement
colours blue and orange
masterpiece artwork natural
Beautiful

In the Stillness
(Elfchen form poems; micro poem hidden)

Submerged
in dreamscapes
where silence reigns
louder than cacophony up
high

Connection
with nature
wondrous and peaceful
this reality here truthfully
rests

Reverie
inner beauty
breathing in stillness
the bottom of the
ocean

Unmasked
facing forward
serene semblance as
future quietens, she dreams
innocence

Submerged high
Connection rests
Reverie, ocean
Unmasked innocence

Mermaid's Paradise

Mother Nature, beauty so pure
Reflected in your eyes azure
Melodious song through lapping water
Eternally grateful that I'm Earth's Daughter

Liquid immersion, another world
Saltwater on lips, sweet kiss is unfurled
Heart beats in sync with wave's song
Symphony of nature where I belong

The ripples of time, the coolness of ages
What will change to this marine life's stages?
Bubbles answer citing no guarantees
... a whisper conservation plea on the breeze

Slip underwater again, a mermaid's paradise
Tempestuous current the only vice
Embrace the wild, sway with the turbulence
Let go of stress and enjoy the impermanence

Sunlight halo, like pure spun gold
Rays woven with aqua – behold!
Bathe in your magnificence, face skyward
Soul is replenished, my heart is inspired

Snowflake
(a Shape form poem)

twisting turning
tumbling   tapering
crystal   cool
clear   capricious
white   wistful
water   wafer

Guardians

The stars are high
each of you are twinkling
Shining your light on each other
love and laughter sprinkling

Waves kissing sand
hear an ocean lullaby
Melting timeless chant
as notes of nature purify

Azure diamonds glint
marine ecosystem sighs
Self-sustaining sea
blending song with darkened skies

They are the Guardians
keepers of air, land, ocean
We respect borrowed time
admire their devotion

The Amnesia Moon

'Twas a moonless night that I was awoken
to a wisp of a whisper flitting past
I knew not what or whom had spoken
yet no fear arose nor shadow was cast

Outside I wandered with a thoughtful heart
gazed up towards the dark berry sky
There, in lush exuberance, not far apart
a dance of constellations performed up high

Twinkling lights of visionary fingers
splashed colour upon charcoal pages of night
Serene winds, a choir of soft singers
dulcet tones accompanying starry flight

I gazed and laughed at the amnesia moon
who missed the midnight sonata's beauty tune

Musical Masterpiece

There's...
...a suspended silence
a held note of expectant breath
right before the first note
of a musical

Then...
...the very first sound of the orchestra
filling the theatre with life
and the beginning of a story
told in voice and music

This...
...my heart beats to
and I'm carried into another world
Actors, attire, sound, set
weaving its art and filling the space

After...
...applause, appreciation, ensemble
and satisfaction
for a visual
masterpiece

II
LOVED ONES

We walk together,
and though we may step away in different directions,
we'll always be connected in our hearts.

My Tribe

My tribe,
I feel you
Gentle
like the sea breeze blowing
on a warm summer day

Wise,
I hear you
Advice
when paralysed at crossroads
and your direction is needed

Beauty,
I see you
Laughter
bubbling on joyful faces
the warm release of true friendship

Life is fulfilled by
the chant of my tribe

As moonlight rises
in the darkened sky
golden dust is sprinkled
upon the shoulders
of dancing sprites

Best Friends

Walk with me
though this crazy life!
Let's sprinkle
pixie dust galore
We'll glow up love
like blossoms in Spring
and laugh till our insides roar

Let's run through
the wild, tangled forest!
We'll face obstacles
thrown in our way
For we are each other's
voice of courage
always united, together we'll stay

I'm free to be me
within your dimensions!
You hold me up and
keep me standing tall
I know I'm safe from harm
My worries are shared because
you're always there, my lucky charm

Grateful for this stroll
down memory lane
You've been in my
beautiful tribe
This crown of hearts
belongs to you
I celebrate our friendship with pride!

Together

As moonlight rises
in the darkened sky
gold dust sprinkles
upon the shoulders
of dancing sprites

They clasp hands
faces shimmering
in the spill of moonshine
and promise a wealth
of future friendship and happiness

Lullaby

Close your eyes, dear child
this breeze
holds your lullaby

Angels' stardust
cast by moon
will change nightmares
into sweet reverie

Sleep…

I'd wished upon a star
and it sent me
you

Brand New Bub

Little babe, my little babe
we've only just met
yet the love that I feel for you
can't be measured yet

Little bub, my little bub
I took your tiny hand
and silently promised you
the best life in this land

Little guy, my little guy
your eyes were squinchy closed
but when you opened them to look at me
the love inside me rose

Little sweet, my little sweet
your roly poly lips let out a cry
and I knew that I would love you
until the day I die

Little one, my little one
although you can't yet say
this unspoken bond we have
grows stronger every day

Little son, my little son
you've opened a brand-new door
Kisses and hugs from your Mummy
we're a family now, forevermore

Fly

Up, my pretty butterfly, up
You'll fly like you were born to do

Let me buoy the wind under you
No one should ever clip your wings
Together we'll sprinkle moonbeams
Encourage hope and love anew

You'll fly like you were born to do
Up, my pretty butterfly, up

Rays to Raise

When I pronounce the word—
Rays
I recall when I first saw you
Baby, your smile shone like the sun
uncontained by the night

When I pronounce the word—
Raise
my son, I swore to do the best by you
so you grow into your own self

When I pronounce the phrase—
Rays to Raise
as the clock hands tick by
I know now it's time
to lift you up
so you can fly

Alphabet Baby

Awake and aware, angelic appearance
Before breakfast, beginning barefoot, battleground baby
Childlike commanding, crafting considerable courtly consciousnesses
Deftly defying disillusionment, defending dynamic determination
Exacting eminent engagement, effortless eager empowerment
Friendly frolicking friendship, focused forward freely
Gracefully grounded, guiltless giving glowing glee
Hounding hugs, heralding happiness, hope, honesty
Indulging in increasingly insistent invasion
Jiggling, joking joyous jewel
Knowing knowledge, kneel kindly kid's kingdom
Let lyrical laughter light life limitlessly!
Mum minding miniature man, metering mischief
Noting notorious nonsense, needs nourishment!
Obliging, offering oatmeal, offensive objection, output overboard
Patiently picking plate, punishment provided
Quickly querulous, questioning quibble
Rapidly reacting, revealing ripping rambunctious roar
Sanctimonious sizeable screams, serving sentiments shown
Tempestuous thermonuclear toddler tantrum, torrent tears
Unroll unrest, undertake unification
Vanquished violence, viewed victoriously valentine
Woven welcomed warm whispers
Xiaosaurus!
Youngster yawning
Zzzzzzzzzzzzzzzzz...

First Day at School

Mummies - Part 1

Mummies crying at the school gate
holding on to little hands

Trying hardest to be brave but
realising time's like sand

Off they go now, new loose uniform
too big hats for their little faces

Wave goodbye now, time to go now
heartstrings travel with their babes

Kindy Teachers – Part 2

Teachers' ready, hearts are steady
classroom's prepped for little gems
Mind's refreshed, our eyes are clear and
stamps are inked for our new friends

Kids are safe here
Please have no fear dear
we'll take care of your precious kids

Wave goodbye now
Time to go Mum
Trust us, we'll take care of them

An Original Masterpiece

Each stroke, original
not to be repeated
Layered composition
never to be deleted

Annoyance flares, attitude
different generation
Reign impatience
change my narration

She's cement, stubborn
strongly opinionated
I'm backing down
disaster's alleviated

Magenta red, gone
replaced by ocean blue
Tide's retreated
nothing to pursue

Look deeper, inside
mother's rainbow light
Me too quick to judge
her heart's alight

Experience splashed, life
knowledgeable wise
For us, her kids
she did prioritise

My mother, masterpiece
step back, admire
Many facets to her
this original, I aspire

My Mother Divine

There she sits
frailty slightly brushing by
Gracefully ageing
woman beautified
Each wrinkle etched
tells a story of times

A fulfilling life lived
within those lines
Once confidence bloomed
now less self-assured
due to circumstances
and hardships endured

Now I'm older
I look at her and see
a mix of Oak and Cherry Blossom tree

My heritage
of strength, love and beauty
devotion not from filial duty

Admiration, gratitude, for she's mine
Approbation to my Mother divine

The Unicorn Messenger

Oh, carry these wishes homeward bound
to the women who deliver life
Let not the weight of fondness weigh you down
nor be distracted from journey's strife

Unicorn magic so soft and serene
Passes swiftly through trails of purple half moons
Moving and flowing through stars and terrene
These words of emeralds, sing a love tune

Sweet Motherhood, love's biology song
delivered before the orange moon sets
Entrusted message to where it belongs
from these grateful daughters with no regrets

Through starlit night,
she delivered in dream
This message of love,
sweet tune agleam

Dodgem Daddy

Cocooned in the car with her Dad
he and her,
seatbelts tugging tight

"Sweetheart," he says, "ready to zoom?"
Heart beating,
excitement, feeling light

Music
Bells ring
Pedals ready?
It's a glorious go and—
Smash!

Dodgems!
Got 'em!
Spare me, please—
BUMP!

Memories of childhood love
coming back in a flash!

Daddy

Tower of strength
no counterfeit advice
Hoist me up onto your shoulders
Papa

Missing You, Dad

Love looks not with the eyes, but hearts
that dwell sustained through timeless past
We're wrapped in love as memories sieve

You're not here
but you live, you live

Moments collected from childhood
Oh precious times from fatherhood
Into angels' embrace, we give

You're not here
but you live, you live

Though someday, somewhere, hand-in-hand
We'll meet once more in our heart land
Last goodbyes were not combative

You're not here
but you live, you live

Grandpa

Your love flows like an endless bank
generous and loving
story time man
Wise one

Saolre **(Life)**
(Written in Traditional Irish Ballad form c1600)

There is a man more complex than we see
saolre saolre saolre
There is a man more complex than we see
living a simple life

He built his strength as he grew
saolre saolre saolre
He built his strength as he grew
living a simple life

As a babe, he travel'd 'cross ocean seas
saolre saolre saolre
As a babe, he travel'd 'cross ocean seas
living a simple life

As a boy, he held up fists to defend
saolre saolre saolre
As a boy, he held up fists to defend
living a simple life

As a rebellious teen, he held snooker cues
saolre saolre saolre
As a rebellious teen, he held snooker cues
living a simple life

He brandished a racquet but it felt like a sword
saolre saolre saolre
He brandished a racquet, but it felt like a sword
living a simple life

His mouth displayed wit as quick as his hands
saolre saolre saolre
His mouth displayed wit as quick as his hands
living a simple life

He is the man who explored the world
saolre saolre saolre
He is the man who explored the world
living a simple life

Whilst others stayed tethered, he took some risks
saolre saolre saolre
Whilst others stayed tethered, he took some risks
living a simple life

A successful business, he cultured and grew
saolre saolre saolre
A successful business, he cultured and grew
living a simple life

His family remain the roots that bind
saolre saolre saolre
His family remain the roots that bind
living a simple life

Through all weathers passing, his storm has calmed
saolre saolre saolre
Through all weathers passing, his storm has calmed
living a simple life

Wooded grains on his face tell a tale
saolre saolre saolre
Wooded grains on his face tell a tale
living a simple life

There is a man more complex than we see
saolre saolre saolre
There is a man more complex than we see
living a simple life

The Family Dog

I just want to fit
into my very own family
where I'm loved completely
for just being me

I don't ask for much
just a cuddle or two
a scratch and tummy rub
lotsa attention from you

I talk to you
with pleading looks and a yelp
if my tummy's hungry
or when I need some help

My tail wags wildly
when my leash comes out
It's my favourite thing
without a doubt!

Talk to me, play with me
leave me never
I'll be your best friend
and I'll love you forever

III
LOVE, SET, MATCH

Come nestle deep in my heart
for this is where you truly belong.

You Belong

Ache…

Hurry home
I miss you, my love

My ears strain
to hear your key
turn in the lock
which tells me

Your travels are done
and you're home
safe

A Love Letter From A Dusty Chest
(an Interlocking Rubiayat form poem)

Milady, I'm compelled to write in haste
after the dance, your face I can't erase
A glance I took, then you stole my whole heart
Blood, muscles gone; atoms of you replaced

Long to navigate your eyes, map a chart
To immerse, drown in green, ne'er apart
My fingers ache to touch your velvet skin
Instead I write, delivered by horse cart

Thus words of ink rest upon paper thin
my earnest hope captured deep within
"Will you be swayed to come to me by moon?"
Galaxy's blessings, our life will begin

The Orange Grove

Follow me
into the orange grove
where birds will hear our laughter

Wander hand in hand
where the smell of fresh citrus
reminds us of spring

Accompany me amongst the saplings
where the sun will witness
our first kiss

*We'll begin our new love
on this fruitful soil*

Tuscan Vineyard

Venus smiled upon Earth

As each ray of sunshine pricked
the barren soil
she laughed in delight
for love budded
in shapely mauve bubbles

When they were ready
she blessed the grapes
with true love
knowing when plucked
from vines ripe

Every drop has Venus' blessing

Man or Wine?
(a Palindrome form poem)

Man or Wine
attractive
bold
complex
romantic and sweet
sometimes warmth
grateful memories
miss you

perfectly oaked, aged to perfection

you miss
memories grateful
warmth sometimes
sweet and romantic
complex
bold
attractive
Wine or Man?

Perfectly Paired

Just you and me
a bottle of grappa—
it's a simple life

Love grows around vines
Sun twists through
and fills space

Paired
with the smile of you
We are a perfect match

Jade

If time was a commodity
I'd trade almost all of it
to disappear with you
be undaunted and free

Every
second
is
precious

You and your
jade stained eyes

This Moment

Time froze
when our eyes locked together
The wind ceased
and stars watched

It was at this moment
that I knew
you were
mine

Flutter

You skipped river stones
across the ocean of my heart
I felt ripples of love
form and settle
deep in my soul

Whispers

I turned my face
to yours
and in that moment
you were the soft spring wind
blowing whispers
of summers to come

Snow Hut

Ice crystals silently float down
from a cloud of white
Around us
the restless wind sings a song
Our noses
not yet frostbitten but cool
demand warmth
The snow hut beckons
with the flickering of red embers
and the promise of schnapps

I take your hand and lead you inside

I Found You

Somewhere in this world
I knew you were out there
So confused was I to find you
Too colour blinded, to find my pair
Noise, busyness, overwhelmed
by expectations of society
Belonging to all yet none
pushed and pulled
by whose proprietary?

Then I met you
and the world went still
you cleared away
my commotion
My vision calmed
yet my heartbeat raced
Locked eyes, joined hands
you have my devotion

L'amore **(Love)**

Love resides deep in my heart
it nestles and snuggles within
A teeny, tiny imaginary part
fitting together like a long-lost twin

Love's humble, doesn't demand air
or attention-seek in this world
When needed, we simply become aware
of warmth as it begins to unfurl

Love spreads up and around;
from home in heart, to head and toes,
bringing joy, heading outward bound
'till lips a smile it does expose

A smile, a giggle, tinkles the air
as connections are formed and made
Then words become a bridge to repair
any past hurts come out of the shade

Love
you're welcomed here
on my lips, my eyes and
in my heart

Meant to Be, You and Me

Consider our world one golden ring
circumstance crisscrossed with chocolate string
When marshmallow stars start to climb
the string vibrates to the cool wind chimes

Although life's lines make an internal maze
through busy lives you meet my gaze
In that moment under the dripping moon
your sugar plum eyes make me swoon

For you're
the pepper to my salt
A single touch
bursts heart to halt
I'm the olive
to your Martini
You're the champagne
to my Bellini

No matter how busy life can be
our dreams connect us together, I see
As we dance, chocolate strings untwist
as Cupid approves our innocent kiss

Loved Being In Love
(a Loop form poem)

I have loved being in love
Love has brought me joy
Joy experienced like nothing before felt
Felt exhilaration for my man, my kids
Kids, my love, who are an extension of me
Me entwined in this world of beauty
Beauty which I will miss
Miss when I'm gone from here
Here I lie, no regrets
Regrets at the end are pointless
Pointless when I'm about to leave
Leave I must
Must I?
I have loved being in love

One Heart

Reveal your life's treasure trove
hiding away behind the sunset
Though my heart is my own
my bellame
this love shared
I don't regret
Our differences are fire and snow
yet we're twin stars moulded from one
We are the makers of magic
greedily lapping gold from the sun
We will plant seeds for
the gardens of tomorrow
and angels will shine on our love divine
No mirage, the truth is transparent—
two hearts beating in sync
no deadline

Gently
(a Palindrome form poem)

Moonlight slips in
gently along winding cracks
soft velvety curtains drawn
slightly apart centre
moonlight slides in
love carried along
twinkling and sparkling
floating each luminous beam
reaching you sleeping
delivering messages of

blessings

of messages delivering
sleeping you
reaching beam luminous
each floating sparkling
and twinkling
along carried love
in slides moonlight
centre apart slightly
drawn curtains velvety soft
cracks winding along gently
in slips moonlight

Perfection

We don't need much
except human connection
Things can fall away
but
you
are
my perfection

Rollercoaster of Love
(a Pantoum form poem)

Remember that feeling of love
That *look* that caused a smile
Stars that shone from high above
Quickened heartbeats all the while

That *look* that caused a smile
It made you feel so high
Quickened heartbeats all the while
A curious rollercoaster of why

It made you feel so high
that sudden loss of air
That curious rollercoaster of why
My heart he did repair

That sudden loss of air
Stars that shone from high above
My heart he did repair
Remember that feeling of love

Cupid's Love Cocktail

Head in the clouds, nubivagrant
as alchemy starts to enchant
Hear wisps of heartbeats in small nips
as Cupid's love potion decants

I sipped love's cocktail and met him
my asterin heart did not dim
Like a lighthouse calls to her ships
an angel's blessings filled to the brim

Morning arose with sunrise lips
we forget time as the hour slips
The meeting of soulmates fated
celebrating as eyes eclipse

Monochrome gone, bright created
blossom and bone, integrated
Cloudhead grounded, I'm elated
love's home now, amalgamated

First Kiss

Memories stir at the end of the pier
listening to the ocean's rush, rolls and peaks
Love's sweetest soundtrack floated on near
where youth's beauty touched the bloom in our cheeks

Your mellifluous laugh filled the night sky
each perfect note illustrated your grace
Encouraged by gold twinkling starlight's sigh
I reached for you, heart beating its own pace

Hand to cheek; your skin, your lips I did crave
waiting and wound up with fiery nerves
Playing it cool but my body betrays
praying for angels to approve and observe

Our lips connect, releasing energy—
sparking darkness into a light syzygy

The Shape of My Heart

He asked me,
"What is the shape of your heart?"

And I answered,
"My heart is outlined
with islands of sand
The shape shifts as I explore
adventures unplanned
I've got diamonds sparkling
out of blue caves
Laughter and tears
singing in ocean waves
Love's freedom
allowing immersion true
Heart's sea tides
washing up treasures from blue
Inside my heart
beats the galaxy of stars
encapsulating exuberance
of our memoirs

The shape of my heart
is the ocean, land, sky dome
The shape of my heart
holds you in its home"

The Colours of You

If I could paint butterfly wings
I'd capture the colour in your eyes
Your hair, the raven's feather brings
a stunning black that emphasizes

Your smile I'd borrow from rainbows
You'll see how much this portrait glows
Blushed peonies sweep your cheekbones
but pales compared to your real tones

Connected Through Time

We meet here under the cover of dark
using a notebook and secret's spark
to open the portal for only eight hours
accessing secret magical powers

For I'd risk anything, crossing lines common
to just touch lips and feel our love blossom
This is our time, kindred whispers connect
Skin against skin left real life unchecked

We live for the moment, love inhaling
wanting the fairytale but truth is unavailing
Time slips away, seven hours are gone
Only 60 minutes left until the new dawn

We'll return back into pages
of our own storybooks
until the next portal's opening
where we'll slip through the nooks

Goodbye
for
now...

Starlit Tunes

A few times a year, we're tangled in time
The cosmic Earth splits, our feet on both sides
Our hands connect, how I've ached for your touch
Dream world exists, hidden treasures I clutch

From far away, our souls meet here
Hearts slip together when True Love appears
Thoughts are entwined through sunsets and full moons
The script of us written in starlit tunes

When muted moonlight starts to fade
and sun's tips of rustic burnt orange invade
A desperate urgency to stay close will start
We grasp at shards of time, ripping us apart

Looking to skies for help, magical clues
Shouting demands for me to stay with you!
Selene, Goddess of the Moon heard our plea
"All we own is in your hands!" cried us to she

Selene heard these lovers ill-fated
and she knew how long these souls had waited
With a fist full of stars and from this date
wrote on celestial fabric their fate:

"To be together for eternity"
Now if you look up to Heavens, you'll see –
Two sparkling joined stars forever entwined
For always...
I am his, and he is mine

Dear World

Dear World
your technicolours blind me
delight and excite me!
Looking toward every day
with new playful eyes
What's your surprise today?

I'll greet your expectations
with raw exploration
and genuine appreciation
Throw me a challenge, World!

I'll look beyond barriers
say goodbye to lines that hem me in
that box me in—
I'll lift the pin

I'll catch what you throw
I'll make sure I grow
and breaking free—
off I'll go!

Bonus Material

Poetry Form Creations

Here are Linda Lokhee's own poetry form creations:

Lokheecolours
Poetry Form Rules
It must contain 3 stanzas.
Each stanza must follow the rhyming pattern "aabb" and each line must have 10 syllables.
Choose 2 colours to use in stanza 1, 3 colours for stanza 2 and 1 colour in stanza 1.
#lokheecolours

Lokhee3
Poetry Form Rules
It must contain 3 stanzas and each stanza must have three lines each.
The syllable count is as follows: 2/2/3 with the total word count being 2/2/1 for each stanza.
#lokhee3

Lokheeflip4
Poetry Form Rules
It must contain 4 stanzas and each stanza must have 2 rhyming couplets.
Each stanza must use the same end words, but also flipped around (in reverse) for the next stanza.
The rhyming pattern is as follows: AaBb bBaA AaBb bBaA
Each line should have 8 syllables.
#lokheeflip4

Lokheelow5
Poetry Form Rules
The main theme/title should be placed right in the middle of the poem.
Above the title, there should be 5 lines and each line must contain a total of 10 syllables.
Below the title, you need to represent and place 5 connected words in random order.
Make sure that all end words and the words below the title rhyme.
#lokheelow5

We have included six examples by Linda Lokhee. You may use her hashtags mentioned under each form's rules (whenever you try them) on Instagram so that she can see them too!

Red Devil

(a Lokhee Colours form poem)

Multiple blazes light up night and day
dancing Red Devil's light show on display
Yellow flames sharp, a hot multi-pronged sword
the pleas and prayers left unheard and ignored

Wild heat strangles clouds and sucks all the air
whirled wind changes, bringing black as despair
Desperate to live, the flames weave through the bush
as greenery crisps and chars with red push

Relentless destruction left in its wake
animals flee homes as fire flames take
Eliminated land, collapsed brown wall
echoes of nature are left in ash fall

Believe In Yourself
(a Lokhee3 form poem)

Walk in
feel eyes
Scrutinize

Stand by
watch them
Realize

She can
own her
Confidence

The Ex-Con
(a Lokheeflip4 form poem)

He always chases the sunshine
not wanting to be left behind
His heart's imprisoned in a cage
standing still on his private stage

Biding time for he's at the stage
of trying to remove the cage
Wanting to leave hist'ry behind
by walking towards bright sunshine

But though the bars let in sunshine
they filter from front and behind
lifting dank darkness in his cage
he's still a pris'ner on the stage

Tight locks remain, trapped at this stage
society-judged in a cage
Moving forward, he's still behind
left in the shadows of sunshine

Ocean Angel
(a Lokheeflip4 poetry form)

Gratitude from beyond the deep
the turquoise tides arise from sleep
Trailing behind to catch the wind
my Angel's never underpinned

She rises up, not underpinned
no weight will ever crush her wind
Now she's awoken from her sleep
her strength and power come from deep

For new day dawns out of the deep
the darkness seeps away from sleep
She throws her madness to the wind
for waves to squash and underpin

Forward facing fears underpinned
she barefoot strides towards the wind
Every second she's not asleep
determination from soul deep

Parenting
(a Lokheeflip4 poetry form)

Voices we heard when we were young
encouraged us to bite our tongue
To be aware of manners true
we would obey was all we knew

And then as teenagers we knew
that what we felt and spoke was true!
Friends' opinions would guide our tongue
troubled parents still thought us young

Then we grew and guided *our* young
no censured words came from our tongue
Our pandered kids followed *their* true
spoilt in life for it's all they knew

Wishing for hindsight that we knew
how strength of voices would guide true
Boundaries should have left our tongue
respect instilled amongst our young

Sign of the Times
(a Lokheelow5 form poem)

Retail used to be appreciated
part of community, integrated
when tourists and locals populated
Now a ghost town, shops lie still, vacated
All staff jobs and wages terminated

TOURISM

perforated

          repudiated

    invalidated

         isolated

desecrated

Acknowledgements

Thank you to my fellow creatives, who truly understand the love poetry provides to the writer, as well as to the reader! Your constant encouragement for my poetry writing makes me so happy. Special thank you to Abbey, Zickey, Timi, Ruchka, Jesse Lee, Bryce, Valerie, Sky Rose, Sarah, Jarred, April, Jean, Carlie, Sam, Brenda, Joel, Niels, Geo, Chris, Sonia, Sharron, Heather, Andy, Sana, Joe, Miram, Sharon, Bryan and Mike— by no means a complete list—I could go on and on. I am so honoured whenever my poems are read regularly on the aforementioned poet's Instagram Lives.

To the strong, clever people behind the Publishers, thank you for giving me the opportunity to be a published poet and to learn more about the other side of the book publishing field.

Special thanks to Reena Doss, founder of Ink Gladiators Press, and Austie M. Baird, founder of A.B. Baird Publishing for recognising my poetry and taking my words a step further and into paperback and e-books for the world to read. I am a very grateful writer to have already had a few books published by their companies.

Many thanks to my picture book publisher, Evan Shapiro, co-director of Cilento Publishing, for taking The Sock Monster and The Night Noise under his 'publishing wing'. I'll always be grateful to him for his patience, sound advice and support, especially when I was a debut author.

I'm also grateful to the following poets for accepting my poetry submissions and collating the poetry book anthologies which my poetry appears in. Thank you to Janani, Anupama CN, Aarthi Sampath, Skye Rose Heywood, Valerie O'Callaghan, Reena Doss, Gary, and Amy Turberville.

Thanks to the founder of Poetry Olympics, Rania M. M. Watts for choosing my original poetry form #lokheeflip4 to be a poetry form which competitors used for their submissions into the competition.

Thank you to Sharron Green for also choosing #lokheeflip4 as one of the forms she taught in the Poetix University workshop.

My beautiful cover design logo was created by the immensely talented Creozoe, who has integrated many parts of my book meanings into the design. I am grateful for his insight into the depth of Scattered Syllables. Thank you Creozoe, working with you to create the logo was fun!

Special mention and thank you to Leonie Hawk Belle, for her beautiful cover on Ink Quilled Thoughts and internal book design for Ink Quilled Thoughts and Scattered Syllables.

To the Instagram community of writers who support each other by reading, sharing , commenting and featuring each other's poetry and stories on their Lives — keep cheering for your fellow writers!

Heartfelt thanks to those who have come across my poetry wall and let me know how my words have affected them, for this is the point of words, to connect. You have all encouraged me to keep writing.

Kind thoughts, gratitude and love always to my beautiful family and friends who have read my poetry, listened to my poems, given me constructive feedback and encouragement, and who inspire some of these pieces inside my book.

You'll live forever inside these pages.

Linda Lokhee

@lindalokheeauthor

About The Author

Linda Lokhee is a primary school and special education teacher, children's book author and published poetess. Her favourite place is the beach, either on the sand soaking up the sunshine or surrounded by ocean water *(she's secretly a mermaid!)*. She loves reading but wishes she had more time to read the endless mountain of books piling up. Love of life's beautiful and varied experiences involving her family and friends inspires Linda to write.

She started two community initiatives in 2015—Feel Good Feb (FGF)—to spread kindness to the community as well as Kindness Is Catching (KiC), to get the community involved by providing a KiC Winter Care Kit and Warmies (scarves and gloves) to help homeless people (sleeping rough) be more comfortable during winter.

Currently, she lives in Sydney's Northern Beaches with her husband, two sons and a sweet, gentle dog named Cookie.

Scan the QR code to follow Linda Lokhee at www.lindalokhee.com.

She's also available on the following social media platforms:
@lindalokheeauthor
Instagram | Facebook | Twitter | Goodreads | Amazon
Email: contact@lindalokhee.com

Author's Note

Dear Readers,

Scattered Syllables was written with the hope that my words can relate to you in some way. There are many poems in my book, covering different topics. Life is varied in its beauty and triumphs, as it is also in times of heartbreak and tragedy. We experience many of these feelings over the years and we carry them with us.

We grieve, we grow, we learn. We laugh, we appreciate, we love. Being aware of our emotions lets us ride the stormy times through and appreciate the rainbows of life.

Scattered Syllables doesn't need to be read in the order of poetry laid out in the book. Feel free to flick to any page, depending on what mood you are in. I do, however, recommend that you end each reading with a poem from the "Love" section, as I like to encourage and promote positivity and love in this world.

Thank you for celebrating the ups and downs of this glorious thing called Life through my words and scattered syllables. I am so happy that you are here along with me, reading my poetic meanderings.

It's good to have you along.

Best wishes

Linda Lokhee

@lindalokheeauthor

Other Published Works

Publications with Cilento Publishing
1. The Sock Monster
2. The Night Noise

Publications with Ink Gladiators Press
1. Chapbook - Ink Quilled Thoughts
2. Collaboration with Reena Doss - A Forbidden Love
3. Interview and *Craving Sunlight's Crown* in Capsized: The Pandemic Lockdown (Summer Seasonal Issue #1)
4. Lockdown Perspective & Review of *Craving Sunlight's Crown* in The Fall and Rise of Chimeras (Autumn Seasonal Issue #2)

Anthology Publications
1. *An Original Masterpiece* and *My Mother Divine* in Gratitudes: To Our Mothers
2. *Dodgem Daddy, The Simplest Treasure* and *Life Heist* in Steady Hands: Ode To Our Fathers
3. *Oh, Young Heart, Shadows, Another Chance,* and *True Friendship Never Dies* in Broken Hearts – Healing Words
4. *Flowing Sands of Time* in Ikigai: The Reason For Being
5. *Memories* in Confessions of the Souls Unknown
6. *Representing the seasons of Australia, Spring, Summer, Autumn* and *Winter* in Sun Cycle: Celebrating the World's Seasons
7. *Some Days* in Mind: A Poetry Anthology Exploring Mental Health
8. *The Irony of Silence* in Poetry Pills: A Prescription for Love
9. *A Doggy's Daydream* in Bedtime Rhymes
10. *Sing Me A Song* in The Book of Hope

What Other Authors Are Saying About
Linda Lokhee

Linda has a beautiful and refreshing tone to her writing and poetry. She is never boxed in to one set or style and is consistently looking to expand and challenge her readers to explore the vast schemes of poetry. Considered a master in forms she has created quite a few of her own which I find admirable and impressive. When reading Linda's work, one will always come away with a little extra hope for their day, as she puts a little bit of sunshine into each word she writes.

Abbey Forrest @abbeyforrestauthor
Author of the *Stirred Moments* series, *Outside The Lines: Perfectly Amazing You!* and *Clothed In Dignity: From Shame to Glory*

Linda Lokhee, also known as Mother Of Monsters, is a writer with a wonderful and amazing talent. Her writings, which are always in different styles and formats, are so unbelievably refreshing and heartfelt. You can always find a great deal of love, hope, and positivity in her writings, which makes her an amazing person and writer in herself. I usually make it a point to visit her page at least once a day for my daily dose of positivity and creativity.

Zickey Marya @rumillenial
Author of *Glad To Be Mad*

Tell Us What You Think

Write to us at contact@inkgladiatorspress.com. We might add your comments or reviews on our website as well as feature your Instagram profile. We appreciate your love for reading. Thank you!

We remain at your service,
Reena Doss | Founder & CEO
Ink Gladiators Press®
www.inkgladiatorspress.com